T0080087

FESTIVAL PRAISE FOR ORGAN

Edited by Mark Thallander

About the Arrangers...

FREDERICK SWANN, Organist Emeritus of the Crystal Cathedral and the First Congregational Church of Los Angeles, is Organ Artist-in-Residence at St. Margaret's Episcopal Church in Palm Desert, California. Since 2002, he has been President of the American Guild of Organists. During his long and illustrious career Mr. Swann has played recitals in many of the major churches, cathedrals and concert halls throughout North America and Europe, as well as in Asia and South America. He has also appeared frequently as soloist with leading orchestral and choral organizations. For 25 years Mr. Swann was Director of Music and Organist of the famed Riverside Church in New York City, and held the same title at the Crystal Cathedral for 16 years, where he was chief musician for the Hour of Power telecast viewed by millions throughout the world each week. Also known as a teacher, workshop leader, competition adjudicator, composer and recording artist, Mr. Swann still performs a limited number of recitals each season.

MARK THALLANDER is best known for his long and distinguished ministry at the Crystal Cathedral. Beginning in 1976, Mr. Thallander served as a Music Associate along side Don G. Fontana and Arvella Schuller. He assisted with the television scripting, service programming, and musical guests on their "Hour of Power" show. During his 18-year tenure at the church, he helped coordinate the 1,000 voices for the gala dedication of the Hazel Wright Organ and participated in the 10th anniversary concert. For the 20th anniversary concert, Mr. Thallander performed Vierne's *Toccata on "Hymn to Joy"* and Wider's *Toccata* from the *Fifth Symphony*. He also conducted both the Cathedral Choir and the Summer Choir on many occasions, as well as shared the responsibility of playing the organ for church services and special events. Since that time, Mr. Thallander has served as a Director of Music and Organist at Lake Avenue Congregational Church in Pasadena, taught as an Assistant Professor of Music at Vanguard University of Southern California, Costa Mesa, and recorded two solo CDs of organ and piano improvisations.

CRAIG PHILLIPS is both a distinguished and popular American composer and organist. He holds a Doctor of Musical Arts degree, a Master of Music degree, and the Performer's Certificate from the Eastman School of Music in Rochester, New York, where he studied with the great pedagogue, Russell Saunders. Dr. Phillips has consistently been a featured soloist throughout the country, and in July 2002, he appeared with the Philadelphia Orchestra for a performance of his *Concertino* for organ and orchestra during the American Guild of Organists National Convention. In 2004, he was a judge for the National Competition of Organ Improvisation in Los Angeles. Increasingly in demand as a composer, Dr. Phillips has been awarded commissions from such organizations as The American Guild of Organists and The Association of Anglican Musicians, along with many others. He currently serves as Associate Director of Music and Composer-in-Residence at All Saints' Episcopal Church in Beverly Hills. He is a member of the American Guild of Organists, as well as the American Society of Composers.

FRED BOCK was one of the most recognized and respected leaders in the field of church music. During his thirty-five year career he was a noted composer, arranger, clinician, organist, pianist, choral director, and music publisher. With over 600 compositions and arrangements in print, his works continue to sell to choirs and keyboard players. His anthems have been sung by leading choral groups around the world and continue to be strong sellers many years after their initial release. His Bock's Best piano series has sold in excess of 250,000 copies and remains the definitive series of sacred solo piano collections. In 1976 he served as the Editor of Hymns for the Family of God, a revolutionary, nondenominational hymnal that has sold over 3 million copies. At the time of his death, Fred Bock was Minister of Music at Hollywood Presbyterian Church, where he served alongside Dr. Lloyd John Ogilvie for 18 years. He was also involved in music industry trade organizations, and served as a member of the Writer's Advisory Board of ASCAP, as well as having been repeatedly elected President of the Church Music Publisher's Association.

STEPHEN STURZ has been a church musician since he began to play piano for a junior choir in Bellflower, California at age 10. He had the opportunity to study with multiple accredited musicians at the university level before he moved on to music professionally. Namely, he was under the instruction of Rayner Brown at Biola University, and later, Ladd Thomas at the University of Southern California. Mr. Sturz holds a Master's degree in Music from USC. He has been the organist at Grace Community Church in Sun Valley, California since 1978.

DIANE BISH, concert and recording artist, composer and international television personality, displays her dazzling virtuosity and unique showmanship around the world. Her international television show, "The Joy of Music," combines world-renowned solo artists, ensembles, and orchestras with entertaining, informative narrative, creating an appealing series for people of all ages and musical skill. From famous churches, cathedrals, palaces, museums, and monasteries of the United States, Israel, and Europe, Ms. Bish has produced, hosted, and performed over 180 episodes of the program. She is also seen weekly on the international broadcasts of the Coral Ridge Presbyterian Church, Fort Lauderdale, where as senior organist, she plays the 117 rank Ruffati organ. Also, she is featured on Art Linkletter's weekly "Gloria" program. The sparkling creativity and artistry of Ms. Bish's performances is equally evident in her compositions. Among her works are: *Festival Te Deum* for organ and orchestra, *Passion Symphony* for organ and narrator, and *Symphony of Psalms* for organ, choir, orchestra and voice. She is the most visible organist in the world today with numerous recordings, concerts, and television appearances.

Festival Toccata on "ST. ANNE"

Arranged by FREDERICK SWANN

Begin with full Swell and Great uncoupled. Large 8' reed on Choir or Solo. Pedal: Full without 32', Great to Pedal.

Prepare General

[1] Three contrasting full ensemble sounds, each *ff*, uncoupled
(If played on a two manual organ, chords marked I and II can be played on the same manual)
Pedal: 32' through mixtures, plus Swell to Pedal if needed

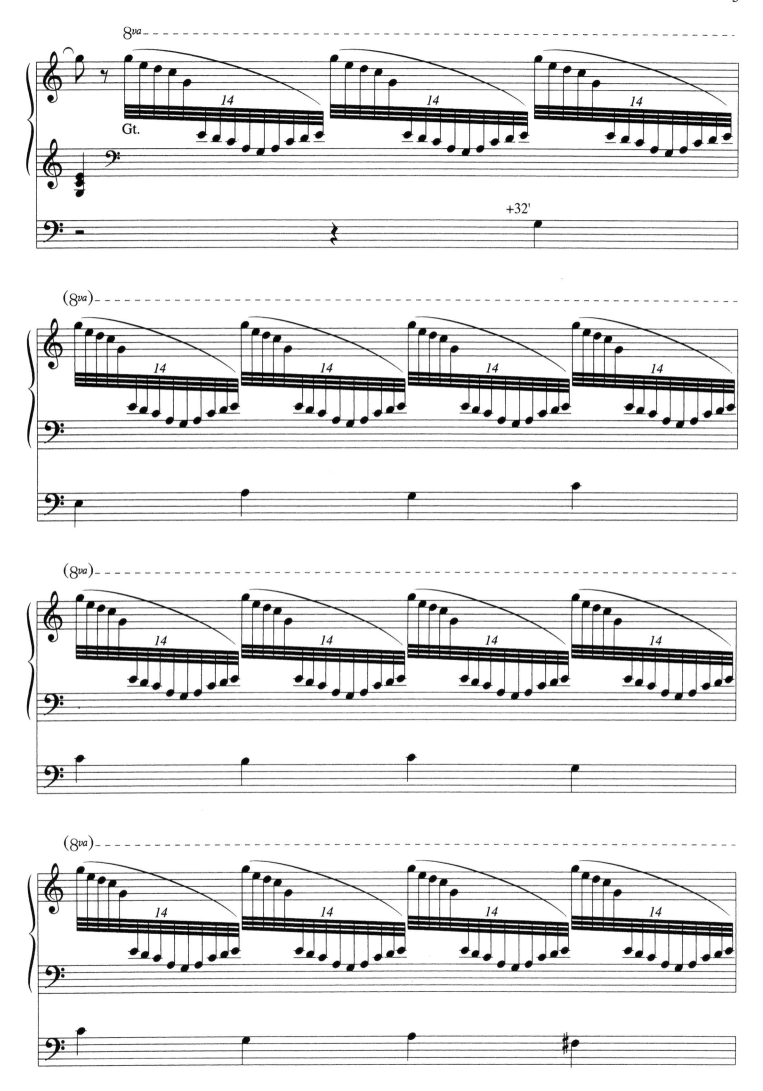

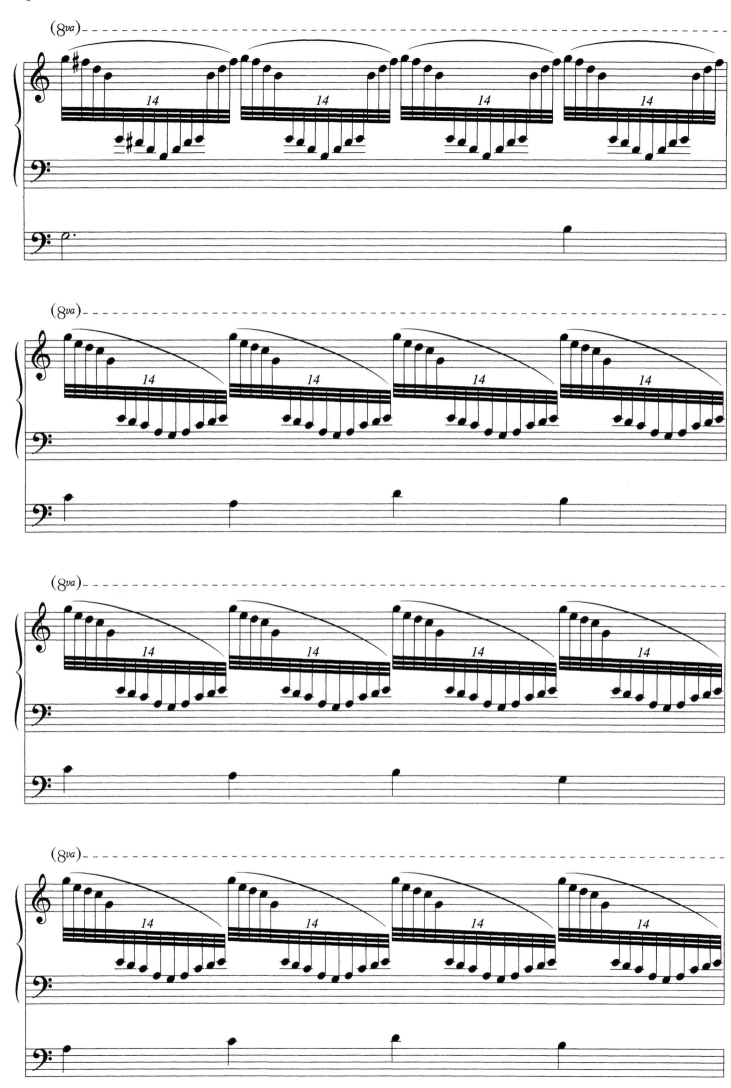

Toccata on "HYMN TO JOY"

Solo: Trompette en Chamade 16', 8', 4'
Great/Swell/Choir: Full to 16'
Pedal: Full, no 32'

Arranged by MARK THALLANDER

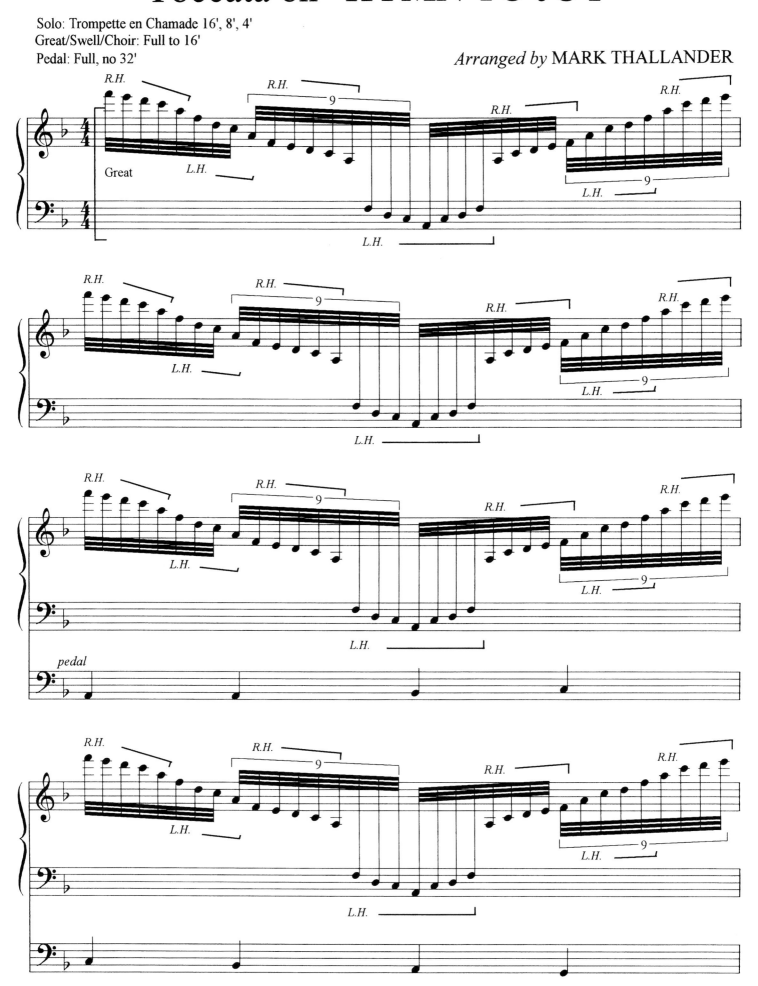

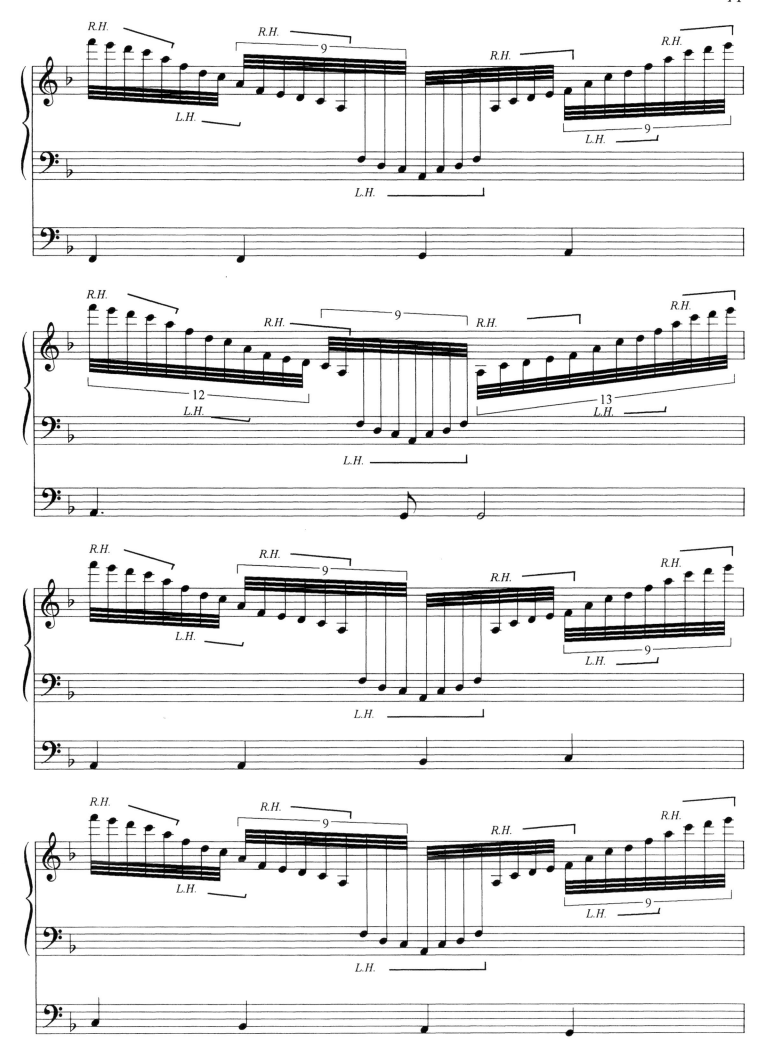

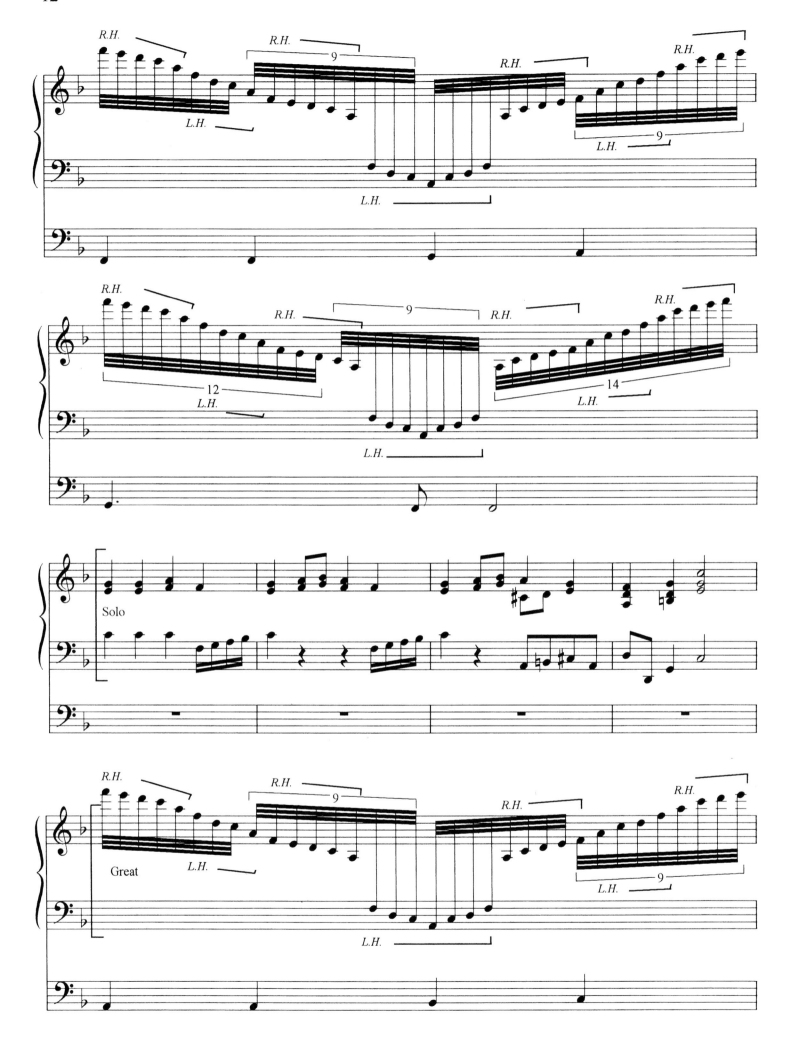

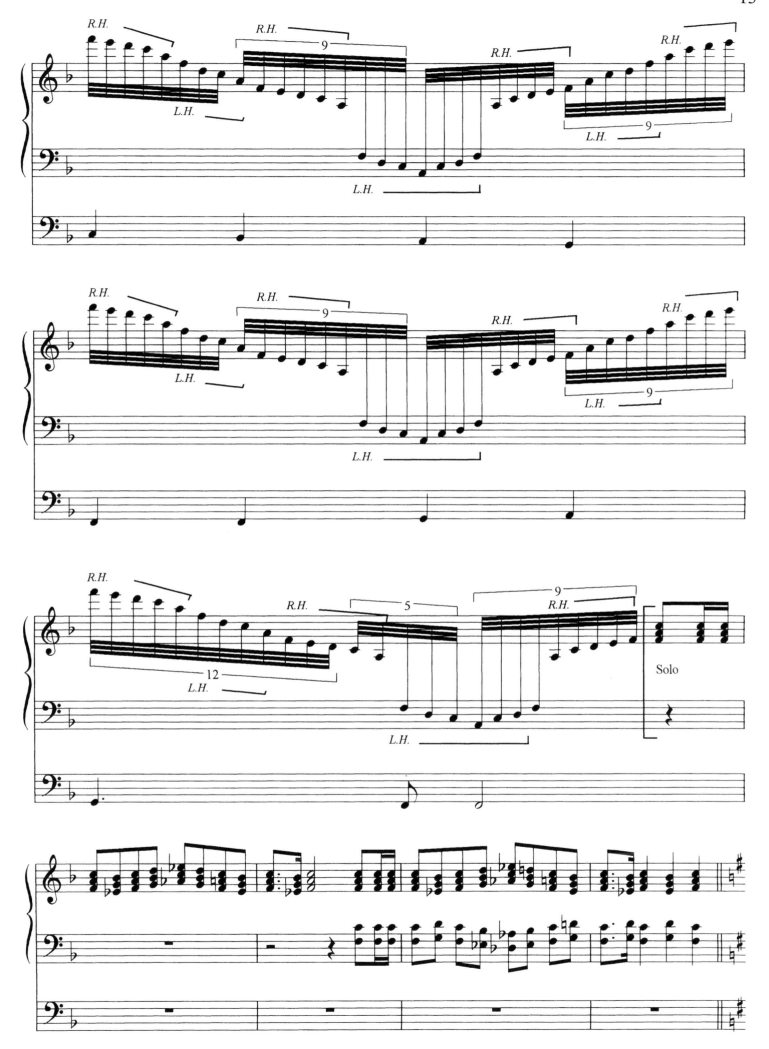

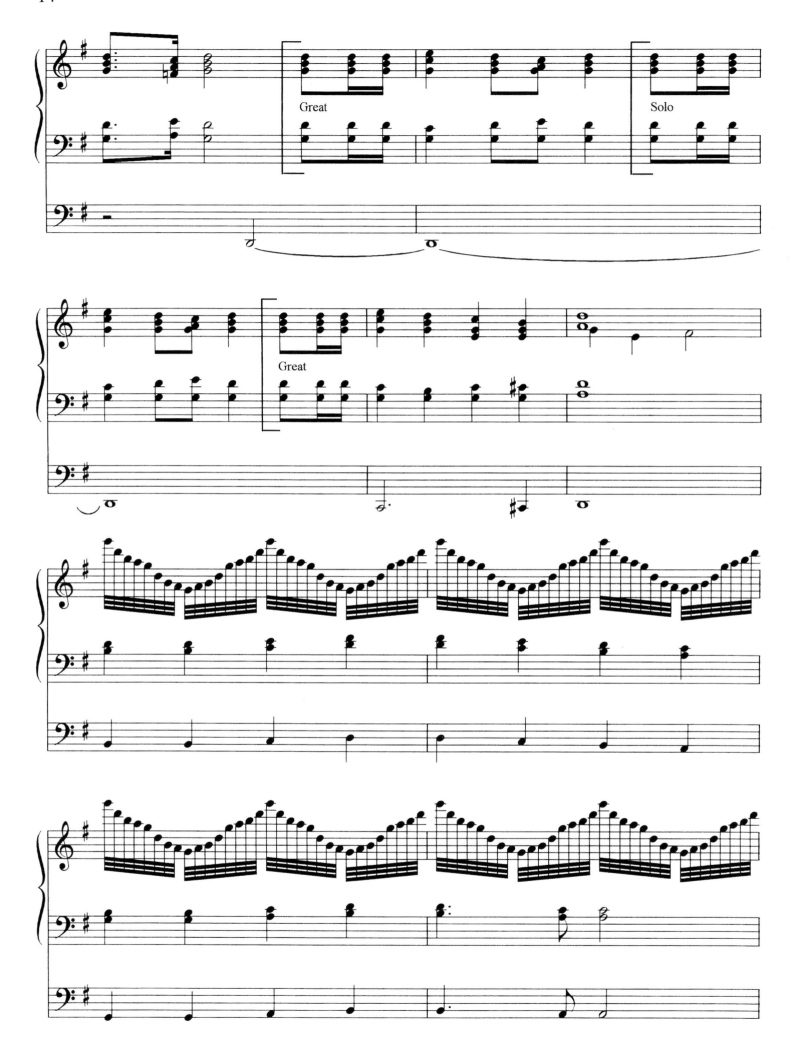

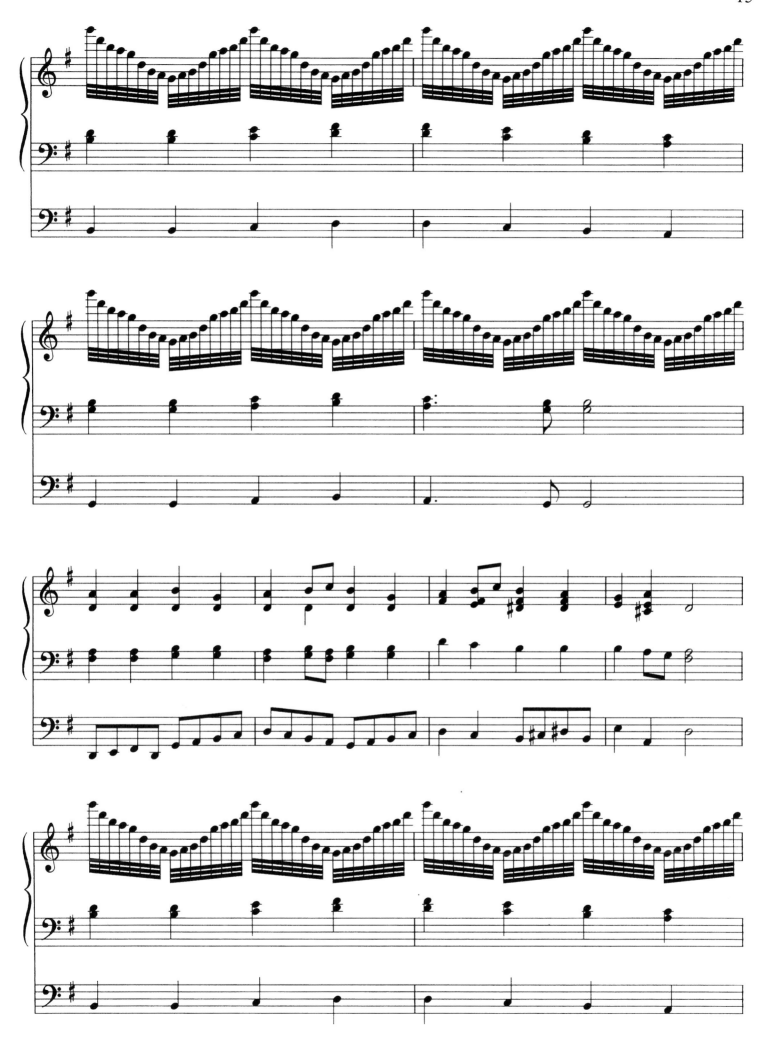

Great

+32' Reed

rit.

Toccata on "LOBE DEN HERREN"

Sw. Full with Reeds
Gt. Full with Reeds; Sw. to Gt. 8'
Ped. 16', 8' and 4'; Sw. to Ped. 8'

Arranged by CRAIG PHILLIPS

Postlude on "NUNN DANKET ALLE GOTT"

Sw. Full organ, light reeds and mixtures
Gt. Full organ, Gt. to Gt. 4′, Sw. to Gt.
Ped. Strong pedal to balance: 16′, 8′, 4′

Arranged by FRED BOCK

Stately and majestically

brilliante

Toccata on "MENDELSSOHN"

Arranged by STEPHEN H. STURZ

Toccata on "EASTER HYMN"

Sw. : Full, Sw. to Ch. 8′ 4′
Ch. : Full, Couplers 8′ 4′
Gt. : Solo Trumpet
Ped. : Full

Arranged by DIANE BISH

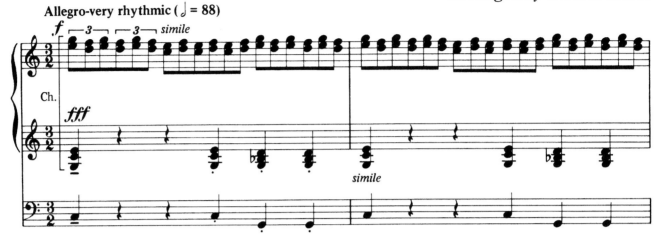

2nd time to Coda

ORGAN MUSIC OF INTEREST AND DISTINCTION
from the Fred Bock Music Companies

Fred Bock Music Company ◇ *Gentry Publications* ◇ *H.T. FitzSimons Co.*
Available at your local music dealer

Adagio (from Third Symphony) (JG0657) . . . . Camille Saint-Saëns/ed. Fred Tulan
All the Things You Are (JG0541) . . . . Jerome Kern/arr. Billy Nalle
    in the style of a Bach trio sonata
American Folk-Hymn Settings (F0623) . . . . Jean Langlais
    Amazing Grace, How Firm a Foundation, Battle Hymn, and three more
Ballade for Organ and English Horn (BG0881) . . . . Leo Sowerby
    (or clarinet, violin, viola)
Century of Czech Organ Music (Vol. 1–F0606/Vol. 2–F0607) . . . . ed. Karel Paukert
Concert Etude (F0634). . . . . Anthony Newman
Expressions for Organ (F0624). . . . . Jean Langlais and Naji Hakim
Folkloric Suite (F0604). . . . . Jean Langlais
Hymns of Praise and Power (BG0705) . . . . Frederick Swann
    accompaniments for 15 congregational hymns
Organ Music of Fred Bock—Vol. 1 Six Hymntune Settings (BG0889) . . . . Fred Bock
    Be Thou My Vision, Morning Has Broken, On Christmas Night, and three more
Organ Music of Leo Sowerby (BG0879). . . . . Leo Sowerby
    Carillon, Pageant, A Wedding Processional, and two more
Rhumba (JG0544) . . . . Robert Elmore
Rhythmic Suite (includes Pavane) (JG0546). . . . . Robert Elmore
Thirty Organ Bridges (BG0702). . . . . Fred Bock
    transition bridges and interludes for service playing
Three Carol Preludes (JG0691) . . . . Richard Purvis
Toccata on "Christ the Lord Is Risen Today" (BG0634). Diane Bish
Trumpet Tune (F0626) . . . . Jean Langlais
    a work for Trompette-en-Chamade
Variants on Hymntunes for Congregational Singing (BG0629) . . . . Fred Bock
    last-verse harmonizations on 14 standard congregational hymns

Gentry Publications

H. T. FitzSimons Company

Fred Bock Music Company